Gemstones, Medallions and Other Pretty Things

Adult Coloring Book

When you share your colored pages online, please include #tabbystangledart.

Find more of Tabby's Tangled Art online:

Facebook: www.facebook.com/tabbystangledart
Instagram: @tabbystangledart
Twitter: @tabbyleann
www.patreon.com/tabbyb
www.sellfy.com/tabbyb
www.amazon.com/author/tabbystangledart

To receive your FREE PDF copy of "How to Color Smooth Gemstones", contact me at tabbystangledart@gmail.com and send me a photo of yourself with this book. The tutorial is very thorough. There are 19 steps in my tutorial which is written for ALL colored pencil brands. I hope you enjoy this book! Please share your colored works with #tabbystangledart or #tabbyb on facebook!

TabbyB

facebook.com/tabbystangledart

facebook.com/tabbystangledart

facebook.com/tabbystangledart

facebook.com/tabbystangledart

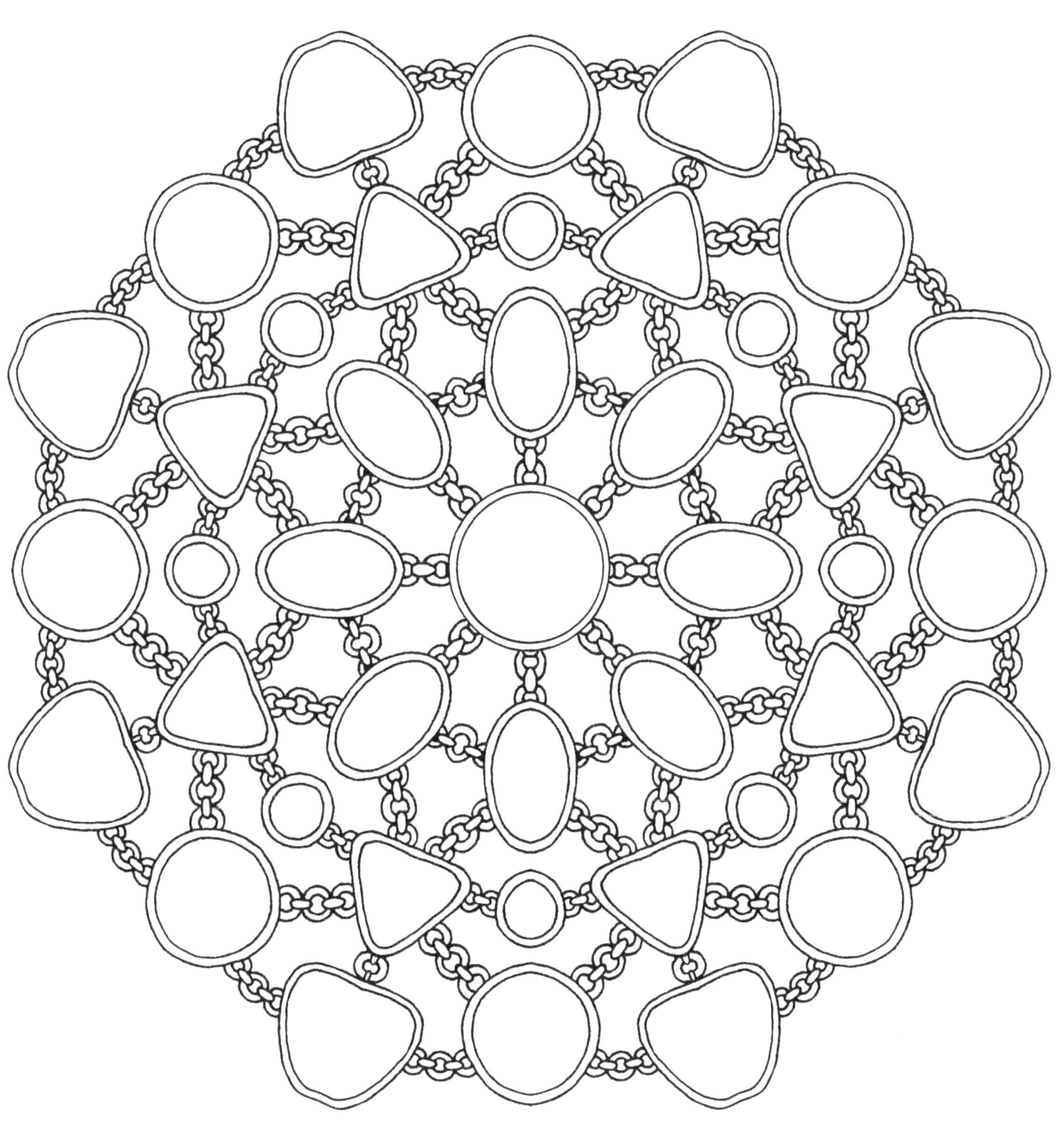

facebook.com/tabbystangledart

©Tabitha L. Barnett 2016

www.facebook.com/tabbystangledart

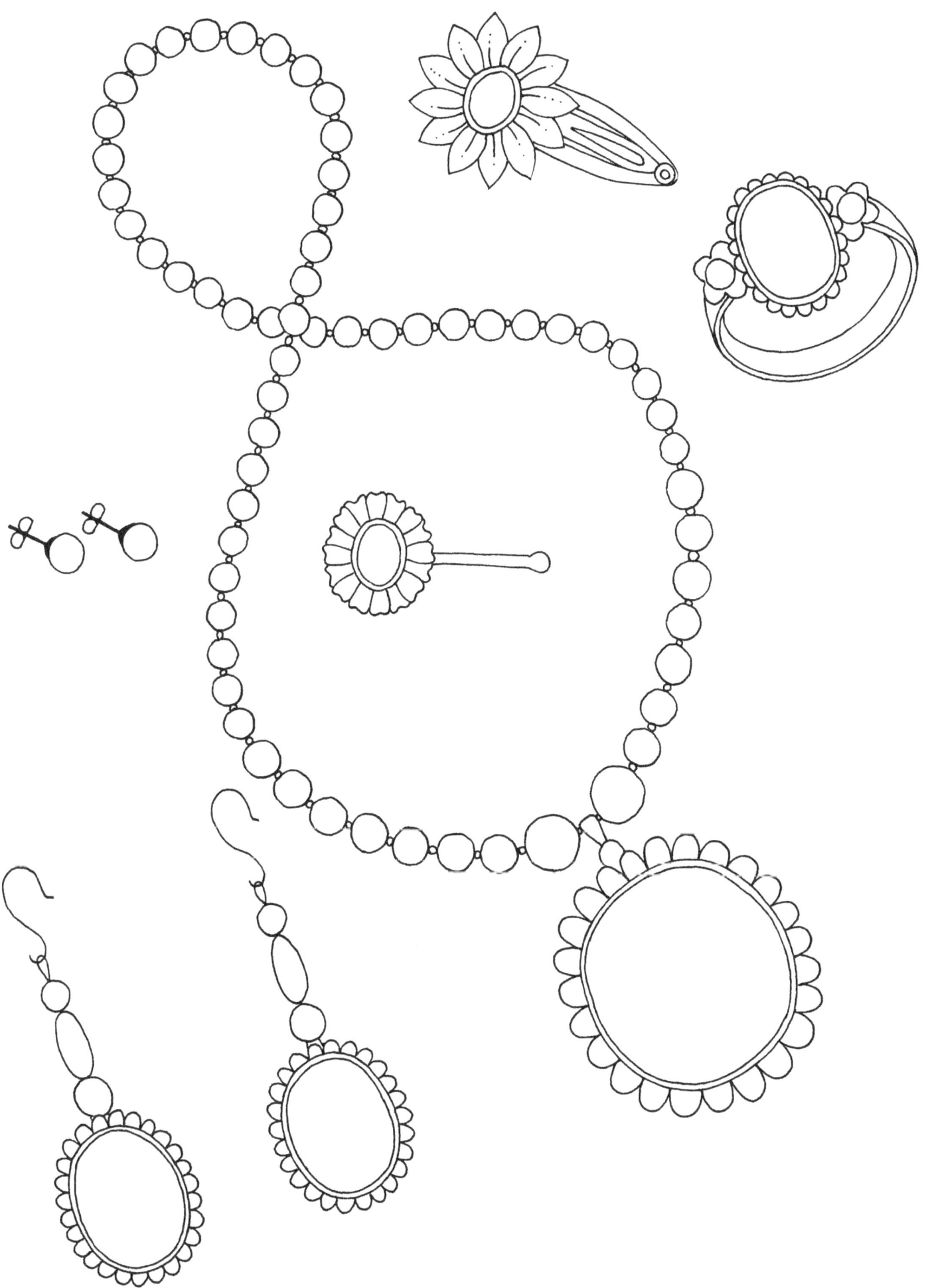

facebook.com/tabbystangledart

facebook.com/tabbystangledart

©2017 Tabitha Barnett

facebook.com/tabbystangledart

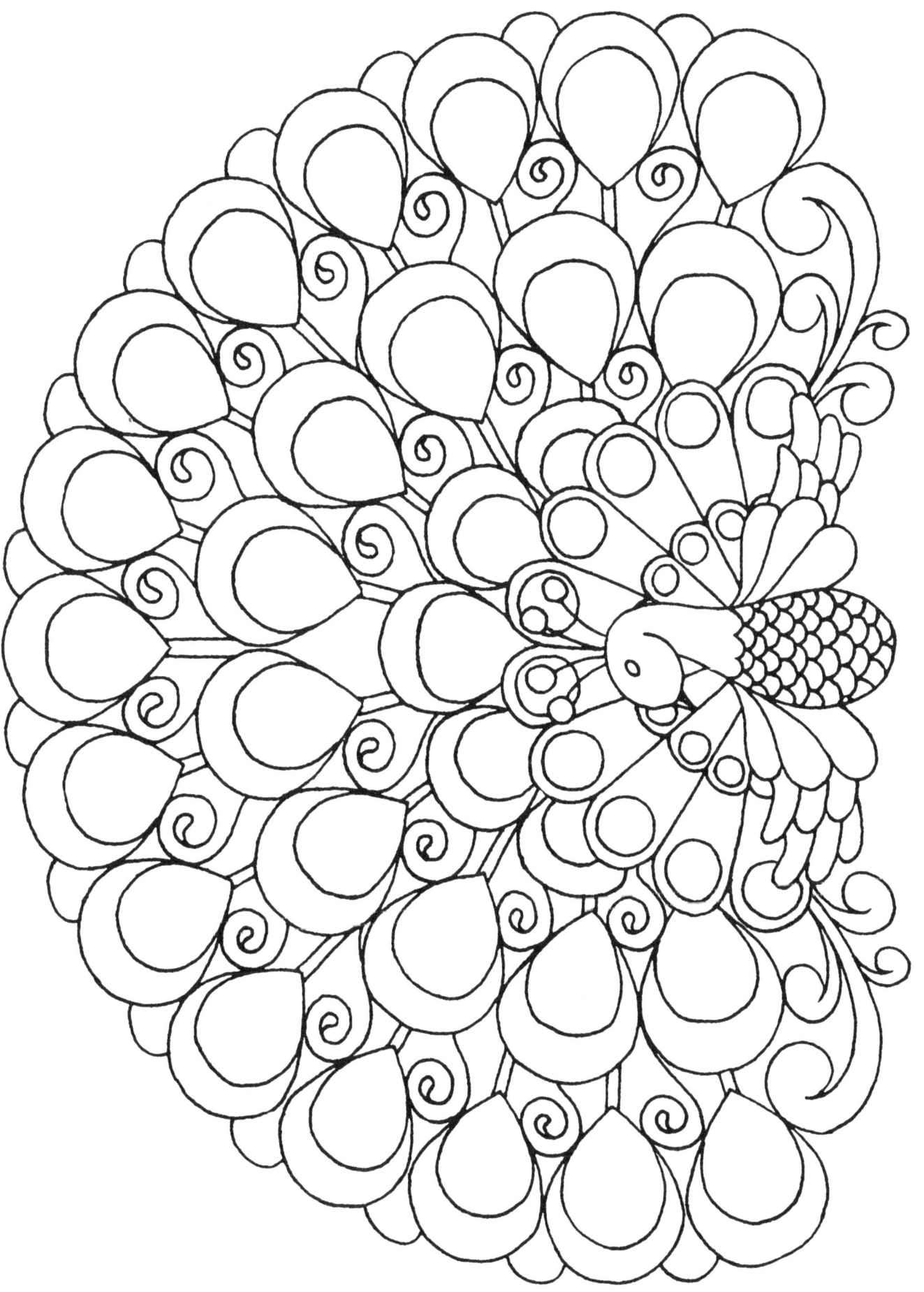

facebook.com/tabbystangledart

www.facebook.com/tabbystangledart

Practice Gem Shapes

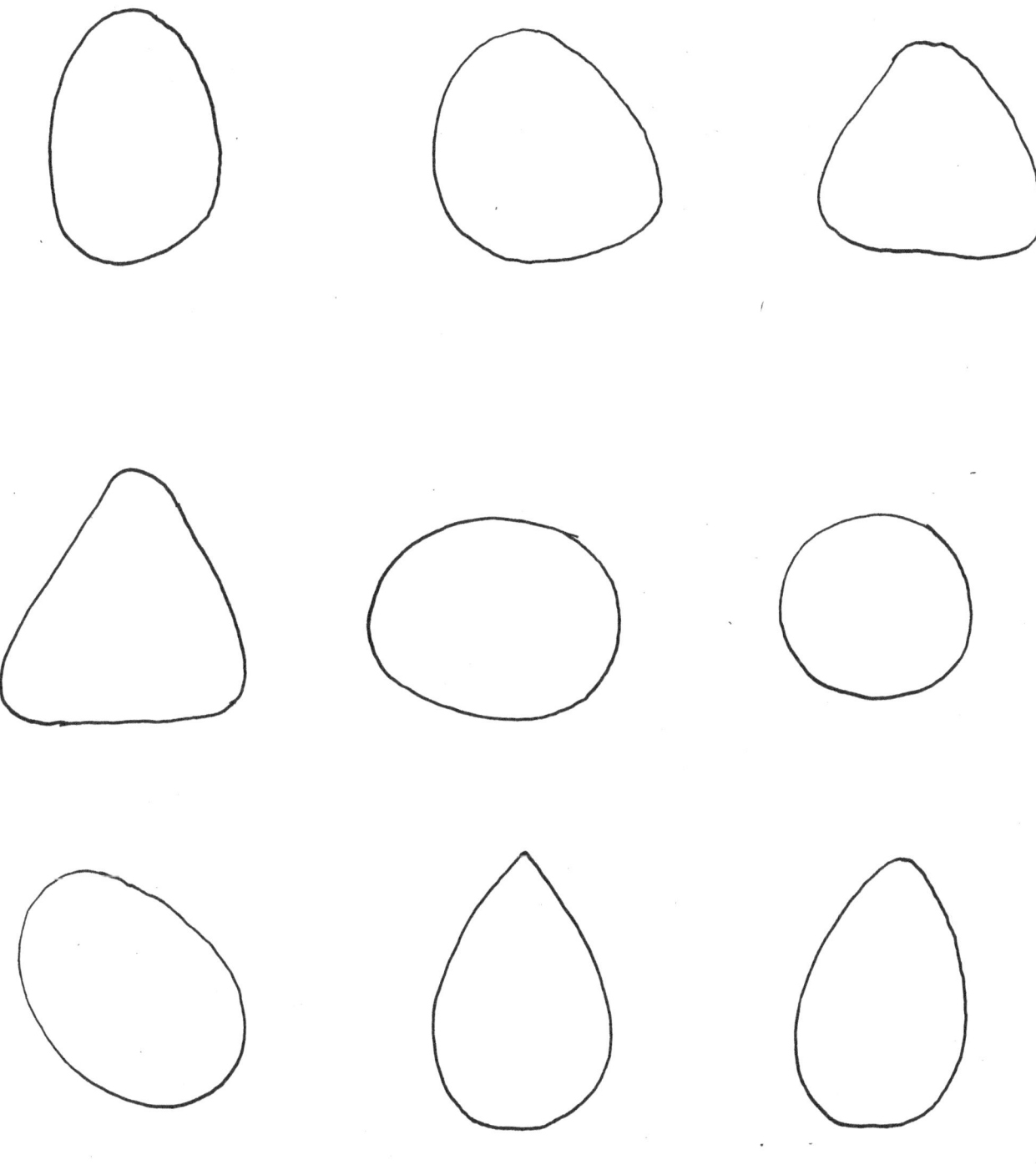

Color Chart

Medium: _____ **Brand:**_____

www.ingramcontent.com/pod-product-compliance
Lightning Source LLC
Chambersburg PA
CBHW081223280526
45787CB00006B/2500